The Sight-reading Sourcebook

Alan Bullard

for
FLUTE GRADES 1-3

Chester Music
part of The Music Sales Group

Published by
Chester Music
8/9 Frith Street, London, W1D 3JB, England.

Exclusive Distributors:
Music Sales Limited
Distribution Centre, Newmarket Road, Bury St Edmunds, Suffolk, IP33 3YB, England.
Music Sales Corporation
257 Park Avenue South, New York, NY10010, United States of America.
Music Sales Pty Limited
120 Rothschild Avenue, Rosebury, NSW 2018, Australia.

Order No. CH67914
ISBN 1-84449-454-3
This book © Copyright 2004 by Chester Music Limited.

Music processing and typesetting by Camden Music.
Original cover design by Chloë Alexander.
Printed in the United Kingdom.

Your Guarantee of Quality
As publishers, we strive to produce every book to the highest
commercial standards.
The music has been freshly engraved and the book has been
carefully designed to minimise awkward page turns and to make
playing from it a real pleasure.
Particular care has been given to specifying acid-free, neutral-sized
paper made from pulps which have not been elemental chlorine
bleached. This pulp is from farmed sustainable forests and was
produced with special regard for the environment.
Throughout, the printing and binding have been planned to ensure
a sturdy attractive publication which should give years of enjoyment.
If your copy fails to meet our high standards, please inform us and
we will gladly replace it.

www.musicsales.com

PREFACE

This book is for flute players of all ages who wish to develop their sight-reading skills, and contains a number of graded exercises which lead up to examples of tests of similar standard to those set by the major examination boards. The precise requirements, and the way in which the sight-reading tests are offered, does vary from board to board so be sure to check their syllabuses and the specimen sight-reading tests that they publish.

However, good sight-reading is not just about getting better marks in examinations: the skill of sight-reading helps you learn all music more quickly and more accurately. It can save you a lot of time!

Sight-reading and learning a new piece—the difference
Learning to sight-read better will help you learn music more quickly, but the approach to sight-reading is not the same as the approach to learning a new piece. When you learn a new piece you often work at it a little at a time, phrase-by-phrase, practising it until it is right. But with sight-reading, the aim is to get it *right first time!* When sight-reading, you *practise in your head*, before you put the instrument to your lips, and when you do start to play, you *keep going* (even if you make mistakes along the way).

Keeping going
This is the most important part of sight-reading, and means that *rhythm*—and counting the basic pulse that underlies it—must be your starting-point. Throughout the book there are sections which are designed to help you with this basic skill—keeping the pulse steady: keeping your internal metronome ticking away in time. The approaches suggested should be applied to all pieces in this book. If you find 'keeping going' difficult, there are plenty of ways to develop it with your flute in its case—tapping the pulse with one hand and the rhythm with the other, tapping the pulse and 'tonguing' the rhythm, counting out aloud while clapping the rhythm, tapping the pulse with the foot while singing, even singing any tune you like *in time* with your feet while you walk along the road!

Getting the notes right and following the shape
Many of the exercises in this book are suitable for singing (in any appropriate octave) so try singing the phrases before playing them, particularly in the early stages: it may not be easy at first but it really helps with imagining what the music will sound like.

Most music moves by step or in small leaps. Good sight-readers don't work out every note: they make sure that they start in the right place and then they follow the shape of the music as they move along. Be brave and try this!

Warm up your brain as well as your fingers
Try *beginning* each practice session with a few minutes of sight-reading: get your musical intelligence working as well as your fingers. Try to imagine what the music will sound like *before* you play it. Don't leave sight-reading to the end!

Try, try again
If you find an exercise difficult, move back a page or two and repeat exercises you have already played. Come back to the difficult exercise with renewed confidence!

Sight-read your way to each new piece
Try the *'right first time'* approach whenever you are learning a new piece. See how much detective work you can do in your head—phrase-by-phrase perhaps—before the flute touches your lips.

The Sight-reading Sourcebook—your passport to saving time and learning more music.

ALAN BULLARD

The Sight-reading Sourcebook for Flute – Grades 1-3

SECTION 1A

Preparing for your GRADE ONE EXAM and for MUSIC MEDALS COPPER and BRONZE

When sight-reading, always begin by working on the rhythm.

Here are some exercises to help.

a) Starting without your flute, count aloud steadily and in time. This is the **pulse**.

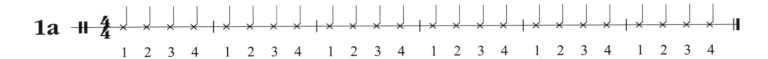

b) Now gently tap the pulse: keep going and when you are ready tongue the **rhythm** out loud.

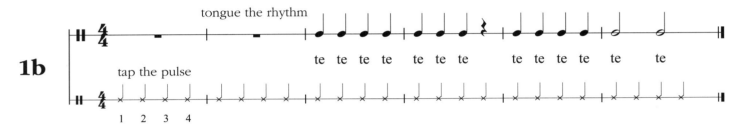

c) Pick up your flute and, counting the steady pulse in your head (gently tap your foot if it helps), play the rhythm on a **single note.**

d) Finally, count the pulse in your head and play the **melody**, following the rise and fall of the notes. Make sure that you **keep going**, even if you make a mistake!

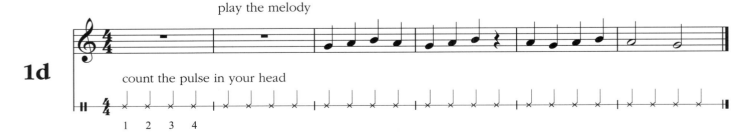

Use the same technique for this exercise, counting the pulse out loud before you start.

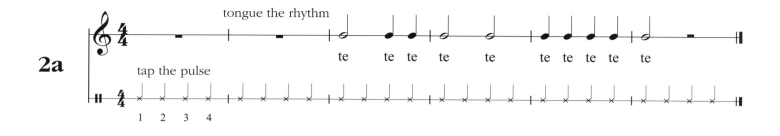

2a

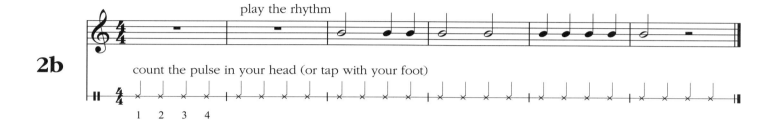

2b

2c

In the exercises that follow:

a) tap (or think) the **pulse** and tongue the **rhythm** (or play it on one note);

b) count the pulse in your head and play the **melody**.

Always count in two bars (in your head) before you start, and **keep going**.

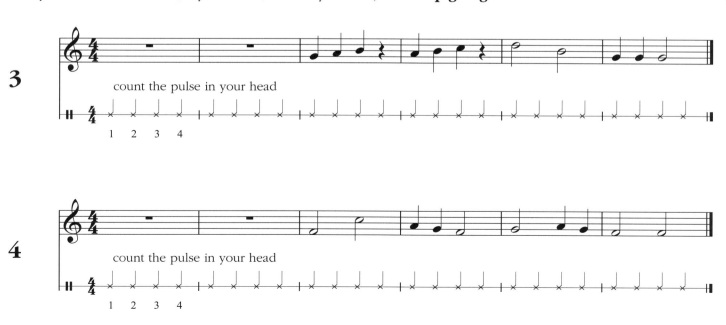

3

4

Remember to count steadily in your head while you play. Once you have started, don't stop!

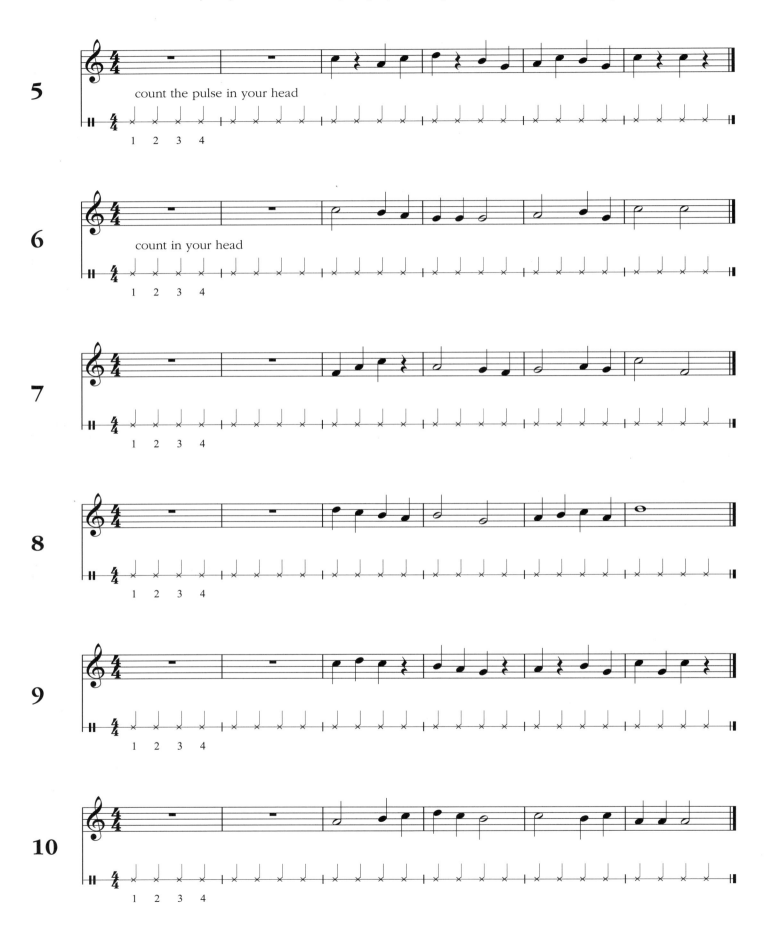

5 count the pulse in your head

1 2 3 4

6 count in your head

1 2 3 4

7

1 2 3 4

8

1 2 3 4

9

1 2 3 4

10

1 2 3 4

Introducing three beats in the bar
As before:

a) tap (or think) the **pulse** and tongue the **rhythm** (or play it on one note);

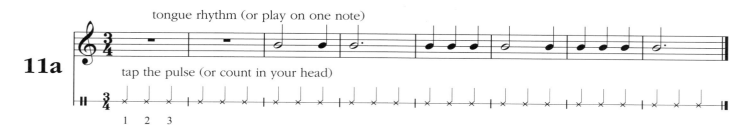

b) count the pulse in your head and play the **melody**. Always 'count in' for two bars (in your head) before you start.

Approach these exercises in the same way.

Introducing quavers

As before, remember to:

    count the **pulse**;

    tongue the **rhythm** (or play it on a single note) while tapping the pulse or counting in your head;

    look at the **melodic shape**.

Then start to play, and **keep going**!

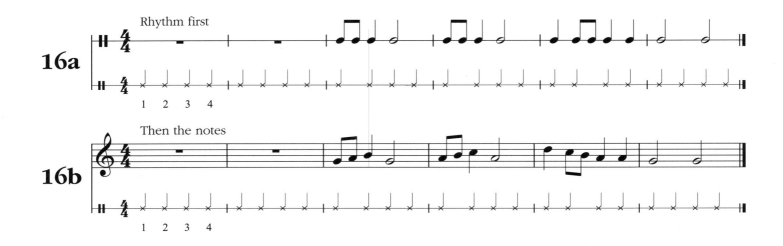

Continue to prepare these exercises in the same way.

13/10/12

Thinking in keys: F major

To sight-read quickly and easily you need to know your way around the flute—that means knowing your **scales and arpeggios**!

Practise the F major scale, slurred and tongued;

and the F major appeggio;

and now play these exercises, looking out for the scales and arpeggios in each. Remember to prepare the **rhythm** in your head before you start to play. Count two silent bars at the beginning and **keep going** steadily.

9

Thinking in keys: G major

Practise the G major scale;

and the G major arpeggio;

and now play these exercises, following the scale and arpeggio shapes. Look out for the **dynamic markings**—the 'louds' and 'softs'.

Thinking in keys: E minor

For some exams you can choose to play either the melodic minor or the harmonic minor scale. But for good sight-reading you need to know your way around both of them!

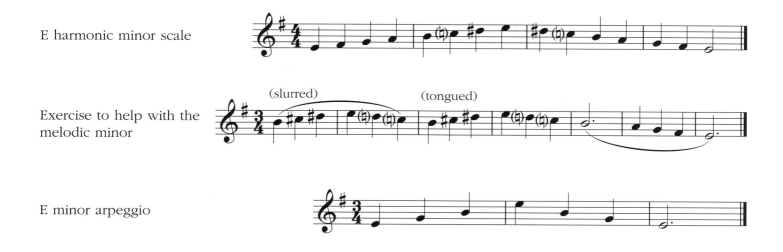

E harmonic minor scale

Exercise to help with the melodic minor

(slurred)　　(tongued)

E minor arpeggio

Look out for the scale and arpeggio shapes—and the sharpened notes—in these exercises.

Sadly

37

p

Steadily

38

mf　　*f*

Rhythmically

39

f

Expressively

40

mf

Smoothly

41

mf　　*f*

Happily

42

f

Now a range of short exercises in the three keys. Remember to:

check the **speed** (and any Italian words)
count the **pulse** and practise the **rhythm** in your head
check the **key signature**, look at the last note to confirm the key, and think of the scale
check the **dynamics**, count two silent bars, and away you go. Don't stop!

SECTION 1B

Sample tests of GRADE ONE standard

Remember that the specific requirements for this level vary between the different examination boards. Some boards allow you a short time to 'practise' out loud. Don't waste this time—be organised!

Check **speed**, count **pulse**, practise **rhythm**, check **key** and **dynamics**. Then when you start to play, count two silent bars, and **keep going**, following the shape of the music.

Is this in G major or E minor? Look at the last note to find out.

Introducing tied notes

Remember to count the pulse and tongue or tap the rhythm, as before. And don't forget to practice the scales of the keys you are playing in!

Look out for the **accidentals** in these exercises.

SECTION 2A

Preparing for your GRADE TWO EXAM and for MUSIC MEDALS SILVER and GOLD
Thinking in keys: D major

Make sure that you know your way around these scales and arpeggios.

Practise the D major scale, slurred and tongued;

and the D major arpeggio;

and now play these exercises, looking out for the scales and arpeggios in each. Remember to prepare the rhythm in your head before you start to play. Count two silent bars at the beginning and keep going steadily.

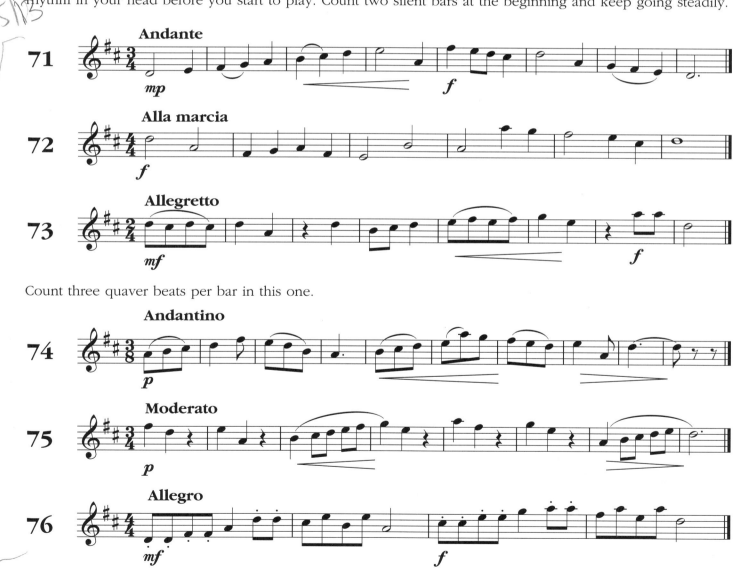

Count three quaver beats per bar in this one.

17

Thinking in keys: A minor

A harmonic minor scale

Exercise to help with the
melodic minor

A minor arpeggio

Allegro

77 *f*

Minuet

78 *f*

Look out for the C sharp here.

Allegretto

79 *mf* *f*

Andante

80 *f* *p* *mf*

Allegro

81 *f*

Andantino

82 *p* *poco a poco cresc.* *f*

Andante

83 *p* *mf*

Introducing dotted notes

Keep counting steadily.
Once you have started to play, don't stop!

84a

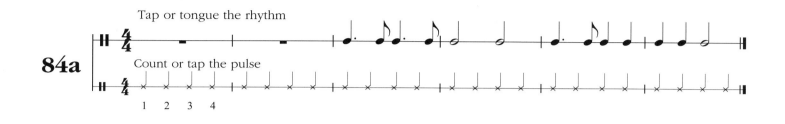

84b

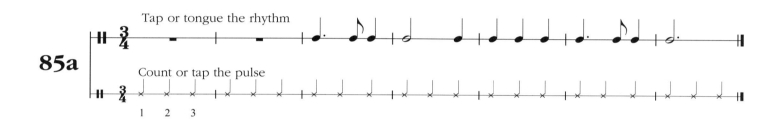

85a

85b

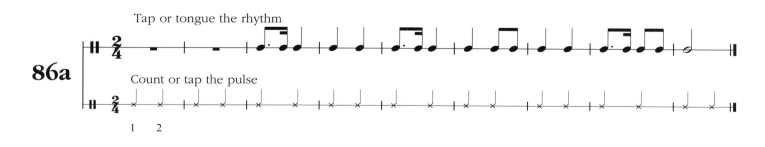

86a

86b

SECTION 2B

Sample tests of GRADE TWO standard

Remember that the specific requirements for this level vary between the different examination boards. Some boards allow you a short time to 'practise' out loud. Don't waste this time—be organised!

Check **speed**, count **pulse**, practise **rhythm**, check **key** and **dynamics**. Then when you start to play, count two silent bars, and **keep going**, following the shape of the music.

SECTION 3A

Preparing for your GRADE THREE EXAM and for MUSIC MEDALS PLATINUM

Thinking in keys: D minor

Make sure that you know your way around these scales and arpeggios.

Practise the D harmonic minor scale, slurred and tongued.

Exercise to help with the melodic minor;

and the D minor arpeggio

Andante
103

Lively
104

Larghetto
105

Alla marcia
106

Andante
107

Allegro
108

Thinking in keys: B flat major

B flat major scale

B flat major arpeggio

109 Alla marcia

110 Gently

111 Allegro

112 Andante

113 Allegretto

114 Andantino

115 Allegretto

Thinking in keys: G minor

G harmonic minor scale

Exercise to help with the
melodic minor

And the G minor arpeggio

Practise the dotted rhythms carefully.

Alla Mazurka

116

Andantino

117

Lively

118

Andante

119

Larghetto

120

Allegro

121

Introducing **semiquavers** and $\frac{6}{8}$ time

SECTION 3B

Sample tests of GRADE THREE standard

Remember that the specific requirements for this level vary between the different examination boards. Some boards allow you a short time to 'practise' out loud. Don't waste this time—be organised!

Check **speed**, count **pulse**, practise **rhythm**, check **key** and **dynamics**. Then when you start to play, count two silent bars, and **keep going**, following the shape of the music.